PETS PLUS

Gerbils and Hamsters

Sally Morgan

W
FRANKLIN WATTS
LONDON • SYDNEY

This edition published in 2013 by Franklin Watts

Franklin Watts
338 Euston Road, London NW1 3BH

Franklin Watts Australia
Level 17/207 Kent St, Sydney, NSW 2000

Created by Taglines Creative Ltd: www.taglinescreative.com
Author: Sally Morgan
Series designer: Hayley Cove
Editor: Jean Coppendale

ISBN: 978 1 4451 1847 5
Dewey classification: 636.9'356
A CIP catalogue record for this book is available from the British Library.

Picture credits
t=top b=bottom l=left r=right m=middle
Front cover: Hamster, Alamy/BP7315; hamster logo Shutterstock/Abel Tumik;
gerbil Shutterstock/Lock Stock Bob; hair Shutterstock/cla78
Back cover Shutterstock/Vishnevsky Vasily
Title page hamster istock/Abelcazar, gerbil istock/Camilio Torres; Contents
gerbil Shutterstock/Simone van den Berg, hamster Shutterstock/Abel Tumik;
p4t Shutterstock/Alex Kalashnikov, 4b Shutterstock/Eric Isseleee ; p5t
Ardea/Andrey Zvoznikov, 5b Ardea/M Watson; p6 Shutterstock/Ingrid
Prats; p7 Shutterstock/Julia Lutgendorf; p8 Shutterstock/Vasily Koval;
p9t Shutterstock/trgowanlock, p9b Peter Mass; p10 Angela Hampton;
p11-Shutterstock/Hintau Aliaksel; p12 Papilio/Robert Pickett;
p13t istock/Kerstin Waurick, p13b Papilio/Robert Pickett; p14
Angela Hampton; pp15 & 29 Shutterstock/Very Olive photography;
p16 Angela Hampton; pp17 & 28 istock/Sarah Bossert; p18l
Ardea/M. Watson, p18r Angela Hampton; p19 Alamy/Maximilian
Weinzierl; p20 Ardea/Ian Beames; p21l Ardea/Ian Beames,
p21m Ardea/Johan De Meester, p21r Shutterstock/
Allocricetulus; p22 Ardea/M. Watson; p23 Ardea/Steve
Downer; p24t Ardea/M. Watson, p24b istock/Abalcazar;
p25 istock/Camilo Torres; p26 Shutterstock/Vishnevsky
Vasily; p27t Shutterstock/Petrov Andrey, p27b
Shutterstock/Eugene Sim; p30 Shutterstock/
Lock Stock Bob; p31 Shutterstock/Hintau Aliaksei.

Printed in China

Franklin Watts is a division of Hachette
Children's Books, an Hachette UK company.
www.hachette.co.uk

Contents

Pet rodents, wild rodents 4

Gerbil or hamster? 6

Buying your pet 8

Welcome to your home 10

Caring for your pet 12

Finding food 14

Handling your pet 16

Wild cousins 18

Giving birth 20

Sense of smell 22

Rodent talk 24

Instant expert 26

Pet quiz 28

Owning a pet – checklist 29

Glossary 30

Index 32

The meaning of the words in **bold** can be
found in the glossary.

pet rodents, wild rodents

Hamsters and gerbils are cute furry animals, and make great pets. They belong to a group of animals called **rodents**.

What's the difference?

Hamsters are slightly bigger than gerbils. They have a small stumpy tail, while gerbils have a long tail. Hamsters like to sleep all day, and are active in the evening and at night. Gerbils are awake during the day. Both hamsters and gerbils have extra-large front teeth for chewing.

▶ Hamsters do not have a long tail like gerbils, just a short stump.

◀ Gerbils have long back legs with large feet, and a long furry tail. They use their tail for balance.

4

Pet or wild?

Pet hamsters and gerbils are the same size and body shape as their wild relatives. However, pet animals have a wider range of colours and hair types. Wild gerbils live in the desert and are light brown. Pet gerbils can be black, grey or even spotted.

Hamster colours

Wild hamsters have dark or multi-coloured coats that help to **camouflage** them from enemies. Pet hamsters have been **bred** to have black, brown, golden and white coats.

▲ In the wild, the colour of a gerbil's fur helps it to blend in with its background.

◀ The pet hamster (left) is light grey and cream. The wild European hamster (below) has a multi-coloured coat that helps it to hide in the wild.

Gerbil or hamster?

 Both hamsters and gerbils are easy to keep. However, there are some differences to think about before you decide which **species** to buy.

Night and day

In the wild, hamsters hunt for food at night when there are fewer **predators** around. In the same way, your pet hamster will sleep during the day and come out only in the evening. Gerbils are active during the day, just like their wild cousins, and sleep at night.

PET POINT
Hamsters are active at night, so it's best not to keep your pet in your bedroom.

▶ Your pet hamster will want to play at night. This could be noisy!

One or more

In the wild, gerbils live in groups so your pet gerbil will not like living alone. You should always keep two gerbils together. Make sure they are the same sex; two brothers or two sisters is best. Many hamsters are not as **social**. The **Syrian hamster** (also called the golden hamster), must be kept on its own as it will fight with other hamsters. **Dwarf hamsters** can be kept in pairs or small groups.

▲ Dwarf hamsters live happily together, but they may fight if a new hamster is added to the group.

Do it!

Gerbils often wink! Scientists do not know why — it could be because they are happy. Try this. Wink at your gerbil and see if it winks back. Give it a treat if it does.

Buying your pet

There are a few things to look for when you go to buy your pet, so you can be sure you get a healthy one.

Shops and breeders

The pet you buy should be between 6 to 8 weeks old. Many pet shops sell hamsters and gerbils, but make sure that the animals' cages are clean. You can also buy your pet from a **breeder**, who should be able to give you advice on how to look after it.

Bright and healthy

When you are choosing your pet, check that it has bright eyes and clean fur. Avoid animals that are skinny or have scabs. You can often tell the age of a hamster by looking in its ears. Young hamsters have tiny white hairs that disappear with age. Older hamsters have no hairs inside their ears.

◄ A hamster that is used to being handled will be more tame and easier to manage as a pet.

Hamster types

There are different types of pet hamster. The most common is the Syrian hamster, which is the largest of the pet hamsters. They are calm and easy to tame but can nip your finger if they are frightened. Dwarf and Chinese hamsters are smaller and can be kept in pairs. Smaller hamsters can be more difficult to handle because they move very quickly and wriggle a lot.

◀ If you've never kept a hamster before, a Syrian hamster will make a great first pet.

Gerbil types

Nearly all pet gerbils are **Mongolian gerbils**. But recently, shops have been selling fat-tailed gerbils, which come from the deserts of North Africa. Fat-tailed gerbils are friendly, active pets that can be kept in pairs or groups.

▲ Fat-tailed gerbils have a short tail with no hair.

Welcome to your home

Getting a new pet is very exciting. Before you bring your pet home, make sure you have everything ready that it will need.

Large home

Many people keep their pets in a wired cage with a deep plastic base. The plastic base is easy to clean, and the wire sides mean that your pet gets plenty of air. Or you could keep your pets in a special tank. Wild hamsters and gerbils live in **burrows** and dig tunnels. Your pet should have lots of interesting tunnels to explore.

Do it!

Checklist — things you will need for your new pet:

- cage or tank
- nest box
- selection of tubes and platforms for inside the cage
- food bowl • water bottle
- toys • **bedding**

▶ In the wild, gerbils and hamsters are very active, so it is best to buy your pet a home like this one, which has tunnels and rooms for them to explore.

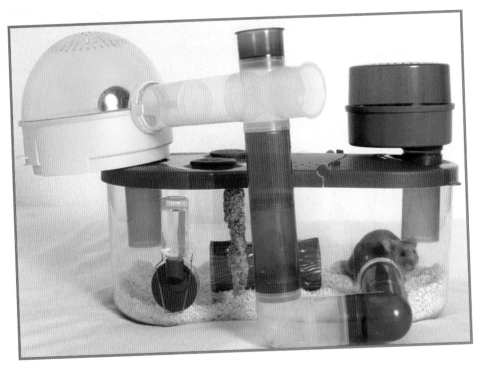

▶ A nest box, such as this wooden one, will keep your pet feeling safe and cosy.

Nesting

Wild hamsters and gerbils make a nest in their burrow where they can hide and sleep. Your pet will also need a nest box. Hamsters and gerbils chew a lot, so they will soon destroy thin plastic nest boxes. A wooden or **ceramic** box is best, or even a clay flower pot. Add some bedding, such as hay or paper towels, that they can **shred**.

PET POINT

Cover the floor of the cage with a thick layer of hardwood shavings. Avoid cedar or pine shavings, and don't use sawdust as this can get in your pet's eyes.

Be patient with your pet

Once you have put your pet into its new home, give it some food and water. But do not try to handle it straight away. Let it get used to you by sitting close to its cage, being quiet and just watching.

Caring for your pet

Hamsters and gerbils are easy to look after, but you will need to spend at least 30 minutes a week doing a few jobs to keep them healthy.

Cleaning

Hamsters and gerbils are clean animals and they do not smell much, but you do have to change their bedding every week. Throw away all the old material and give them a layer of fresh bedding.

Put your pet in a small container with plenty of air holes, while you give its home a good clean. Use soapy water to wash the cage or tank, and also to wipe down the tubes, wheels and toys. Dry everything with a clean cloth before you put your pet back.

◀ Wear gloves when you clean your pet's cage, and wash your hands after you have finished.

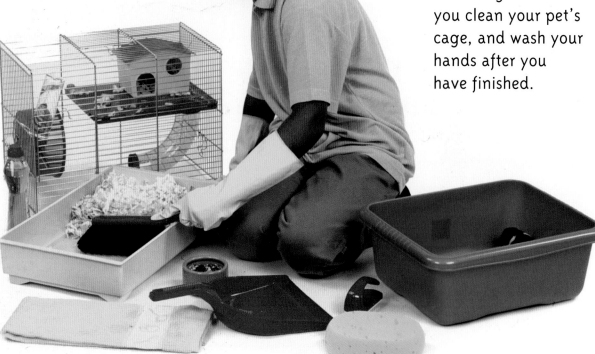

Sand baths

Both pet and wild gerbils love sand baths. Gerbils live in deserts where there is little water. When their fur gets greasy, they clean it by rolling around in sand. You could put a tray of sand in your pet's cage.

▲ This pet gerbil is enjoying a sand bath.

Grooming

Most gerbils and hamsters clean their fur and do not need brushing. However, the fur on some of the long-haired types can get **matted**, so use a small soft toothbrush to remove the tangles. Wild and pet gerbils often **groom** each other. This keeps their fur clean and helps to build friendships in the group.

▶ A soft toothbrush is ideal for grooming your pet.

PET POINT
Gerbils are desert animals and do not drink much water. They produce less urine, so their cages do not smell as much as those of a hamster.

Finding food

 You must give your pet the right food to keep it healthy. Hamsters and gerbils eat a variety of plant foods.

Wild food

In the wild, hamsters and gerbils feed mostly on grasses and seeds. But they also catch small insects, such as moths and beetles. Pet hamsters and gerbils are usually given a ready-made food that contains a mix of seeds. Make sure your pet always has clean water to drink.

▶ Buy a sturdy ceramic food dish so your pet cannot chew it or tip it over.

Pouches

Hamsters pick up lots of food and stuff it into **pouches** inside their mouth so they can carry it back to their burrow. This way they have to make only one trip to search for food rather than several. In the wild, this means they are less likely to be spotted by a predator. Often they store their food to eat later. You may see your pet doing this.

▶ Hamsters (right) and gerbils use their front paws like hands to pick up and hold food.

Handling your pet

Hamsters and gerbils are lively animals and they move quickly. They can be tricky to handle at first, especially the dwarf hamsters.

First steps

If your pet is not used to being handled, start slowly. Don't try to pick it up if it is asleep. When your pet is active, open the door and place a treat on your hand. Hamsters and gerbils are curious animals, so they will creep out on to your hand. When your pet is happy on your hand, stroke it. Only when your pet likes being stroked should you pick it up.

Smelly hands

Wash your hands before handling your pet. If it smells food on your hands it may try to nibble your fingers!

◄ Keep your hand still while your pet climbs on to it and don't make any sudden movements.

Picking up your pet

The easiest and best way to pick up a gerbil or hamster is to **scoop** it up in your hands. Another way is to place your hand over its back with your fingers either side of its head. Be gentle and quiet, otherwise your pet will get scared and may nip you.

PET POINT
Never grab your pet by its tail.

Moving your pet

If your pet does not like being picked up and you need to move it, place a container with air holes in the cage with a treat inside. When your pet is inside the container, pop a lid on and move it out of the cage.

▲ Hold your pet gerbil (above) or hamster gently in the palm of your hand, supporting it carefully underneath — make sure you do not squash or squeeze it.

Wild cousins

Pet hamsters or gerbils are very like their wild cousins in many ways. They love to burrow, and they are active at certain times of day.

Tunnels

Wild hamsters and gerbils dig underground tunnels using their feet. Sometimes they use burrows that other animals have dug. Pet hamsters and gerbils also enjoy digging. Make sure your pet has a pile of shredded paper or bedding to tunnel into. Your pet will also like running through tubes, which are like burrows.

▲ This European hamster (left) is poking its head out of its burrow to see whether it is safe to come out and hunt for food. The pet hamster (right) is doing the same with a toy tube.

Night feeds

Syrian hamsters live in the hot deserts of the Middle East. They sleep during the day and come out to find food after **dusk** when it is cooler. Your pet hamster will do the same.

High speed

Wild hamsters and gerbils are very lively, constantly moving around in search of food. Pet hamsters and gerbils are just as active so they need a large cage and plenty of tubes and toys to keep them busy.

▲ A piece of wood like this makes a good toy and means gerbils such as these can chew on it to keep their front teeth healthy, as well as play.

Gnawing teeth

Rodents have large front teeth that they use to **gnaw** or chew through wood. These teeth continue to grow throughout their life so they have to keep chewing to wear them down. In the wild, hamsters and gerbils chew tough foods to keep their teeth short and sharp. Give your pets a wood block to chew.

Giving birth

Rodents are ready to have young when they are only a few months old. All rodents produce lots of babies.

Nesting

Pet and wild hamsters and gerbils give birth to their babies in a safe nesting place. Wild females make their nest at the end of one of their burrows, which they line with dried grass and even sheep's wool. A pet hamster or gerbil lines her nest box with hay or shredded paper.

▼ A female gerbil is **pregnant** for 25 days and has between 4 and 6 babies.

Life cycle of a Syrian hamster

A pet Syrian hamster is ready to breed when she is about 4 months old. She is pregnant for about 16 days and gives birth to between 5 and 9 babies. Each baby weighs just 3 g and is blind and naked. Within 7 days the babies are ready to leave their nest and explore. They feed on their mother's milk for about 3 weeks. Young Syrian hamsters are ready to leave their mother when they are about 5 weeks old.

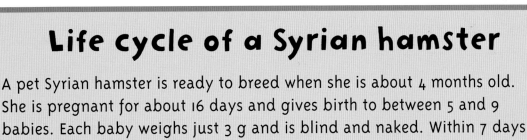

newborn hamsters

2-week-old hamsters

young adult hamster

Ready to breed

Wild Syrian hamsters are ready to breed when they are 5 weeks old, but owners of pet hamsters do not let them breed until they are older. In the wild, hamsters and gerbils breed during the summer when there is plenty of food around, but pet animals can breed all year round. Wild Syrian hamsters live for about 2 years. Pet hamsters and gerbils can live for about 3 years.

PET POINT
It is important to leave a female alone with her newborn babies in her nest for the first week, as she may eat them if she is disturbed.

Sense of smell

Smell is important in the lives of hamsters and gerbils. They **scent mark** to identify each other and to mark their burrows.

▲ Hamsters leave lots of smells around the entrance to their burrow.

Scent marking

Hamsters and gerbils mark trees and rocks with urine as a way of telling others to stay away. Hamsters rub their paws over their ears and face so their scent is transferred to their feet. Then they stamp their feet around the entrance to their burrow, leaving lots of scent. Gerbils have a **scent gland** on their bellies. Male gerbils rub their bellies on their cage or on furniture when they are out of the cage. This leaves a scent that other gerbils can smell.

Smelly trail

The small **Russian Campbell hamsters** travel long distances in search of food. To make sure they do not get lost, they mark their path with scent. Before they leave their burrow, they rub their paws over their head so that they are covered in scent. As they run along the ground, their paws leave a trail of smells that they follow home.

Who are you?

Hamsters recognise other hamsters from their smell, and pet hamsters soon learn to recognise the smell of their owner. A gerbil greets another gerbil by licking its mouth. It identifies the other gerbil from the taste of its **saliva**!

▼ These wild gerbils are saying hello by touching each other's face and mouth. Watch your pets to see if they do the same.

Rodent talk

In the wild, hamsters and gerbils behave in lots of different ways to survive. Your pet may do the same.

Squeaks

Hamsters and gerbils do not have very good sight but they have excellent hearing. They talk to each other by producing **high-pitched** squeaks, which other animals cannot hear.

Danger sounds

Hamsters freeze when they hear a strange sound or noise. In the wild, this helps them to survive because if they stay still they are less likely to be spotted by a predator. Pets can be scared by strange sounds, too, so they should be kept in a quiet place.

▶ Both wild (above) and pet hamsters (below) stay alert and listen for strange sounds when they are coming out of their homes.

Whiskers

Hamsters use their long, sensitive **whiskers** to find their way around in the dark. Both gerbils and hamsters use their whiskers to test the openings of holes and tunnels. Their whiskers are the same width as their body, so if their whiskers get through so will their body.

◀ This gerbil is using its whiskers to find out whether its head and body will fit through the hole.

Thumping

Gerbils warn others of danger by making a thumping sound on the ground with their hind legs. As soon as a group of gerbils hears another gerbil thumping, they run for cover.

PET POINT
Cats purr when they are happy. When your pet gerbil is happy it will feel as if it is **vibrating** when you hold it in your hands.

Instant expert

There are about 25 different species, or types, of hamster, but more than 110 types of gerbil. Gerbils are often called jirds or desert rats.

Rodent homes

Gerbils come from Mongolia and Northern China where they live in deserts and dry **grasslands**, and a few live in the mountains. Syrian hamsters live in the hot deserts of the Middle East, but many hamsters are found in Central Asia where it is not quite so hot. The European hamster lives across Europe into Russia.

▶ **Winter White hamsters** come from Siberia in Russia.

FAST FACT
The Winter White hamster gets its name from the way its coat colour changes to white in winter when there is snow on the ground.

The largest hamster is the European hamster, which is about 34 cm long.

... and smallest

The smallest species of hamster are the dwarf hamsters, which are only 5.5 to 10 cm long. The smallest gerbil is the **Baluchian Pygmy** gerbil, which has a body about 5 cm long and a tail that is longer than its body.

The largest ...

The largest type of gerbil is the Great Gerbil, which comes from Turkmenistan in Central Asia. It is 40 cm long, including the tail.

Dangerous shadow

Syrian hamsters are hunted by **birds of prey.** They soon learn to recognise the shadow of these birds overhead and race for cover.

FAST FACT
The word 'hamster' comes from the German word 'hamstern', which means to hoard or store.

Not a gerbil

The word 'gerbil' comes from the word 'jerboa'. However, there is a small mammal called a jerboa that is not a gerbil!

▲ A jerboa is a small rodent that looks a bit like a mini kangaroo.

First gerbil

The Mongolian gerbil was imported into the USA during the 1950s by scientists. They realised it was an easy animal to look after and it soon became a popular pet.

◄ Some pet Mongolian gerbils have white fur and red eyes.

pet quiz

Now you know a bit more about what is involved in looking after pet rodents, is a hamster or gerbil the right pet for you?

1. **How much time will you need to spend each week caring for your pets?**
  a) Not sure
  b) I don't have any time to look after them
  c) At least 30 minutes a week

2. **How long can gerbils live?**
  a) About 10 years
  b) A few months
  c) About 3 years

3. **What type of cage is best for a hamster?**
  a) A wire cage
  b) A hutch
  c) A large wire cage with a deep plastic floor

4. **Which pet is active at night, gerbils or hamsters?**
  a) Both of them
  b) Gerbils
  c) Hamsters

5. **Is it important to give your pet a wood block to chew?**
  a) Yes, it stops them getting hungry
  b) No, they'll just make a mess with it
  c) Yes, because it keeps their teeth short and healthy

See page 32 to find out if a gerbil or hamster is the right pet for you.

Owning a pet – checklist

All pets need to be treated with respect. Always remember your pet can feel pain and distress – it is not a toy.

To be a good pet owner you should remember these five rules. Make sure your pet:

- never suffers from fear and distress
- is never hungry or thirsty
- never suffers discomfort
- is free from pain, injury and disease
- has freedom to show its normal behaviour

You have to check your pet every day to make sure it has fresh water and food. You must keep its home clean, and make sure that your pet has enough room to move around.

Buy new supplies of food in plenty of time so that your pet never goes hungry. If it is ill or hurts itself you must take it to a vet.

You must never leave your pet alone for more than a day. When you go on holiday, arrange for someone to look after your pet.

Unless you want your pet to have babies, make sure you keep only hamsters and gerbils of the same sex together. If you have other pets, make sure that they cannot harm or frighten your pet hamster or gerbil.

When you let your pet out to play, make sure the area is safe – that there is nothing sharp and no wires for it to chew.

Glossary

Baluchian Pygmy one of the smallest species of gerbil. This species came from Egypt, Morocco, Pakistan and north-west India originally

bedding material that an animal uses to fill its nesting box. Gerbils and hamsters need hardwood shavings and hay, or pieces of paper towels, which they can shred

birds of prey predatory, or hunting birds, such as eagles or owls

bred when young are reproduced or raised

breeder person who keeps animals, such as pet rodents, to breed and sell

burrow to dig a tunnel underground; a series of tunnels

camouflage colouring that helps an animal blend in with its surroundings so that it's more difficult for predators to see

ceramic made from hardened clay, such as china or porcelain

dusk after sunset when it is just beginning to get dark

dwarf hamster a particularly small species of hamster

gnaw to bite or chew with the teeth

grasslands flat plains where there is grass but few trees

groom to clean or brush fur

high-pitched a sound that is shrill or squeaky

matted tangled, often forming into clumps

Mongolian gerbils a species of gerbil originally from Mongolia in Central Asia. Most pet gerbils are Mongolian gerbils

pouches pockets, such as cheeks, that are used to store food

predators animals that hunt and eat other animals

pregnant when a female animal is carrying babies in her body

rodents animals that have large gnawing teeth, for example rats, mice, squirrels and guinea pigs

Russian Campbell hamsters a type of dwarf hamster with thick, woolly fur. They are named after the man who first found them in Russia, W. C. Campbell, in 1902

saliva the liquid in the mouth that makes it easier to swallow food and helps digestion

scent gland part of the body that produces a strong-smelling substance

scent mark to mark territory by leaving a smell. This acts as a signal for other animals of the same species

scoop to pick up in the hand

shred to rip into long pieces

social animals that like to live with other animals of the same type

species a group of animals that have the same appearance, for

example the Syrian is a species of hamster

Syrian hamster the most common type of hamster, also known as the golden hamster. They originate from Syria in the Middle East

urine liquid waste produced by an animal, often called pee

vibrating a regular shaking movement

whiskers stiff hairs found around the nose, used for touch

Winter White hamsters also known as Russian Winter White hamsters. A type of dwarf hamster with fur that turns white in winter. In the wild, their white fur acts as camouflage in the snow

Index

bedding 10, 11, 12, 18, 30
behaviour 6, 7, 13, 22, 23, 25
biggest gerbil 26
biggest hamster 26
brushing 13
burrows 10, 11, 18, 20, 22, 23, 30
buying 6, 8

cages 10, 12, 19
camouflage 5, 30
care 12–13
cleaning 12

digging 10, 18

food 14, 15, 19

gerbil breeds 9
    Baluchian Pygmy 26, 30
    fat-tailed 9
    Great 26
    Mongolian 9, 26, 27, 30
giving birth 20–21
grooming 13, 30

hamster breeds 9
    Chinese 9

dwarf 7, 9, 16, 26, 30, 31
European 5, 26, 18
Russian Campbell 23, 31
Syrian (golden) 7, 9, 19, 21, 26, 31
Winter White 26, 31
handling 8, 9, 11, 16, 17
homing 10–11
hunting 18

jerboa 27

life cycle (hamster) 21
life span 21

nest box 11, 20
    nesting 20
noises 24

play 6, 10, 19
pouches 15, 31
pregnancy 20, 21, 31

rodents 4, 19, 20, 24, 26, 31

safety 11
sand baths 13
scent marking 22–23
sleep 4, 6, 11, 19

smallest gerbil 26
smallest hamster 26
stroking 16

tails 4, 9
teeth 4, 19, 30
thumping 25
tunnels 10, 18, 25

whiskers 25, 31
wild gerbils 5, 7, 10, 11, 13, 14, 18–19, 22, 23, 24
    colour 5
wild hamsters 5, 10, 11, 13, 18–19, 22–23, 24
    colour 5
    nesting 20

Pet quiz - results

If you answered **(c)** to most of the questions then a gerbil or hamster could be for you.